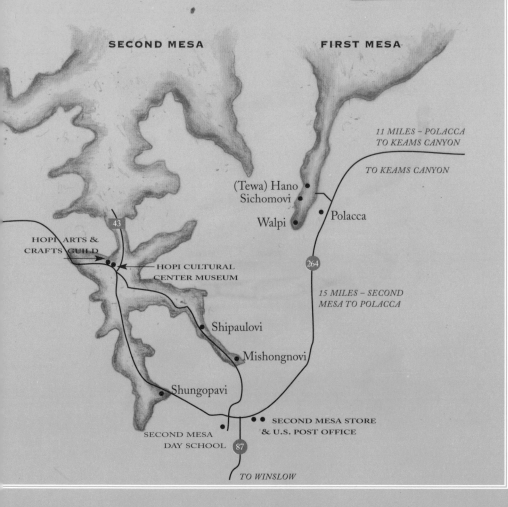

SECOND MESA

FIRST MESA

11 MILES – POLACCA
TO KEAMS CANYON

TO KEAMS CANYON

(Tewa) Hano
Sichomovi
Walpi
Polacca

264

43

HOPI ARTS &
CRAFTS GUILD
HOPI CULTURAL
CENTER MUSEUM

15 MILES – SECOND
MESA TO POLACCA

Shipaulovi

Mishongnovi

Shungopavi

SECOND MESA STORE
& U.S. POST OFFICE

SECOND MESA
DAY SCHOOL

87

TO WINSLOW

JOURNEY TO HOPI LAND

To my grandchildren
    —ANNA SILAS

Rio Nuevo Publishers®
P.O. Box 5250, Tucson, Arizona 85703-0250
(520) 623-9558, www.rionuevo.com

Unless otherwise credited, all photographs show items in the collection of the Hopi
Cultural Center Museum, photographed by Robin Stancliff and © Rio Nuevo
Publishers. Photos on pages 2-3, 7, 13, 34, 43, 46, and front cover © Jerry Jacka.
Shown on page 1: Water serpent kachina; pages 2-3: Sunset at village of Walpi,
First Mesa; front cover: Water Maiden Dance, Second Mesa.

Design: Karen Schober, Seattle, Washington.

            Library of Congress Cataloging-in-Publication Data

Silas, Anna.
Journey to Hopi land / Anna Silas.
      p. cm. — (Look West series)
ISBN-13: 978-1-887896-99-3
ISBN-10: 1-887896-99-6
1. Hopi Indians—History. 2. Hopi Indians—Rites and ceremonies. 3. Hopi
Indians—Social life and customs. 4. Hopi Indians Reservation
(Ariz.)—Social life and customs. I. Title. II. Series.
E99.H7S54 2006
979.1004'97458—dc22

                        2006011509

Printed in Korea.

10 9 8 7 6 5 4 3 2 1

JOURNEY TO
HOPI LAND

Anna Silas

LOOK WEST
SERIES

RIO NUEVO PUBLISHERS
TUCSON, ARIZONA

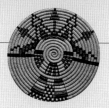

‖ THE HOPI PEOPLE ‖

ASQUOLI!

THAT IS MY GREETING

TO YOU AS WE BEGIN OUR JOURNEY.

IN THE HOPI LANGUAGE IT MEANS

"THANK YOU."

A journey to Hopi Land will take you to a beautiful, cultured place far away from big cities and much more ancient. Located on the Colorado Plateau of northeastern Arizona, the reservation of the Hopi Tribe contains 1.6 million acres of land at elevations from 4,700 to 7,800 feet. Hopi Land is a high, sunny desert where in summer the average high temperature is 87 degrees F, and in winter the average low temperature is 18 degrees F. Making the most of

LEFT: Young Hopi women (Edward S. Curtis, c. 1904). ABOVE: Coiled plaque, Second Mesa.

only ten inches of rain and snow a year, the Hopi have lived here and preserved their intricate culture and their spectacular villages for well over a thousand years. So our journey is a journey through time as well as space.

It is also a journey through the Hopi Cultural Center Museum at Second Mesa, the source of most of the illustrations in this book. Although only a small part of the life of the Hopi people can be shown in a museum, the items shown here are representative of the material aspects of Hopi life. Each of these items expresses, in different ways, relationships in the social and cultural heritage of the Hopi.

The Hopi people trace their history in Arizona back more than 2,000 years, and their history as a people many thousands of years longer through migrations from the south. Their legends tell of a great flood and other events dating back into prehistoric times, which mark the Hopi culture as one of the oldest living cultures in documented history.

The Hopi are composed of clans. They are a deeply religious people. The Hopi religion not only teaches a life of peace and goodwill; Hopi people live it. A few Hopi have converted to Christianity, but most Hopi people continue with their ancient, highly refined culture.

The Hopi by nature are farmers, and they practice a fascinating kind of "dry farming." In these traditional farming practices, fields are not usually plowed, but "wind breakers" are placed in the fields at intervals to retain soil, snow, and moisture. The Hopi have special methods for planting arid fields, where they raise corn, beans, squash, melons, and other crops.

Farmer Leslie Koyawena with melon.

Exquisite arts and crafts created by the Hopi people include pottery, basketry, weaving, jewelry making, and wood carving and painting. The carved figures known as kachina dolls are representa-

Hopi cornfield (Emry Kopta, c. 1912–22).

tive of sacred spiritual beings—beings never to be revealed to individuals who are not initiated into kachina society. Kachinas are supernatural beings. Hopi also refer to them as spirits of their people, to whom they pray for their needs, happiness, health, life, and rain. They also are the spirits of animals and insects. All of these spirits come to visit Hopi Land in the form of clouds. They are very special and important to Hopi people.

Walpi rooftop, drying peaches (Jo Mora, c. 1904–06).

Hopi music includes kachina chants, religious chants, social dances, and lullabies. Song is the spontaneous expression of the Hopi people. It may be heard at all hours, rising from the Hopi villages or from the surrounding desert plains and cliffs. The planter seeking his field at dawn, the woman at her task, the child at play, all sing as naturally as the bird on the bough.

‖ THE HOPI VILLAGES ‖

The twelve Hopi villages are located on the tops or at the feet of three mesas, called First, Second, and Third Mesas, which project out from the huge Black Mesa to the north like fingers.

First Mesa is about twelve miles east of the Hopi Cultural Center, and the village at the foot of First Mesa is called Polacca. There are three villages on the top of the mesa—Tewa, Sichomovi, and Walpi, which is the most spectacular of all the Hopi villages. Terraced into a narrow rock table, with cliff-edge houses and scenic views, Walpi appears unchanged for centuries.

Second Mesa villages are three miles east from the Hopi Cultural Center, which is also located on Second Mesa. The mesa-top villages here are Shungopavi, Shipaulovi, and Mishongnovi. Below

Mishongnovi Village is the tiny settlement of Toreva, where the Hopi Guidance Center is currently located. Shungopavi is considered a mother village. It was the first settlement in this area, previously located below the present Shungopavi Village. Some religious and ceremonial activities originate from this village. Shipaulovi was the last village to be established on the mesa top. It was founded after the Pueblo Revolt of 1680, in order to save the Hopi from

Village of Hotevilla, Third Mesa (Edward S. Curtis, 1912).

possible Spanish reprisal. At the beginning, this village consisted of people from most of the clans. Later many of the clans moved back to Shungopavi Village, and few clans remain today at Shipaulovi.

Third Mesa is a short distance further west, and here are the villages of Kykotsmovi, Old Oraibi, Bacavi, and Hotevilla. The Third Mesa villages are newer communities that branched off of Shungopavi, including Old Oraibi, best known for wicker basketry. Forty miles west of Third Mesa lies Moenkopi, a branch of Old Oraibi that was first established as a farming village, long before the villages of Hotevilla and Bacavi. Later, a permanent settlement was established here. Lower Moenkopi still has strong religious and ceremonial ties to Old Oraibi.

THE HOPI CEREMONIAL DANCES

Each Hopi village has a plaza where ceremonial dances are performed today as they have been for centuries. The portions of the ceremonies that are held in underground ceremonial chambers called *kivas* are for tribal members only. Kivas to the Hopi are like churches to Christians. The yearly kachina dances begin in the kivas in February.

From time to time, outsiders are permitted to observe public ceremonial dances in the plaza, which start shortly after sunrise on weekends and continue intermittently throughout the day, with

Water Maiden Dance, Second Mesa.

> The purpose of our ceremonies is not to be considered a commercial entertainment but a ceremonial attainment: namely, for the attainment of good life and for an abundance of rain. Our dances are not performed for fun events, like the state fair or other public event, as they might be in the white man's world; no, they are much more than that; they are the very essence of our lives; they are sacred.

breaks for lunch and rest periods. The ceremonies usually end at dusk. At times several of the villages hold dances on the same day, giving visitors an opportunity to witness parts of several dances by spending a few hours at each village.

As expressed in the dance, the Hopi communicate with the Creator. The ceremonies are sacred, and sometimes private, and there is no intent to convert outsiders to the Hopi doctrine.

‖ THE HISTORY OF THE HOPI PEOPLE ‖

The Hopi are an agrarian desert-dwelling people. These "peaceful" people, as the name *Hopi* translates, live within a culture rich in tradition and based largely on farming as a way of life. This, however, is only observing the surface. To truly appreciate the Hopi people is to gain an insight into the dynamic and often colorful history of a people surprisingly independent from many other cultural influences.

ANCESTORS

The Hopi people trace their ancestry through the Ancestral Puebloan, Sinaguan, and Mogollon cultures, as well as their predecessors, the Basketmakers. Materially and economically, these ancient peoples were very similar to the modern Puebloan peoples (including the Hopi) who, according to many archaeologists and other scientists, have continuously inhabited the greater American Southwest since approximately A.D. 1. According to Hopi oral tradition, these cultures were ancestral kin groups, who developed independently after the Great Exodus from Mexico. This exodus led to the migration and eventual establishment of the Hopi homeland.

The prehistoric cultures were in transition during their entire existence, constantly moving and adapting to their environment. The common characteristics of all these peoples, all utilizing the kiva structure and same economic mode—subsistence farming of maize— have led many Hopi to believe that they are intricately linked to these ancient people. This is evidenced by events that occurred more than

700 years ago. In the latter part of the thirteenth century, an extraordinary migration took place. It was instigated, scientists say, by intense drought and other climate conditions. This agrees with Hopi oral tradition, which refers to this event as the "Gathering of Clans."

THE HOPI HOMELAND

Over the next few hundred years, these ancestral kin groups, often referred to as clans, concentrated their communities in the area now occupied by the Hopi people. The villages they founded helped form the society that is known today as the Hopi culture. The areas and villages no longer occupied have become part of a tangible chronology to the Hopi and are regarded as shrines, or sacred areas, that mark their original territory. These sacred lands are still utilized in the hunting and gathering of ceremonial articles and for pilgrimages. This land was considered the homeland of the Hopi hundreds of years before the first Europeans arrived.

The Hopi homeland borders the eastern rim of the Grand Canyon and continues northeast to Navajo Mountain, Utah, then southeast toward Lupton, Arizona. From there the border continues southwest to the Apache Descent Trail, along the Mogollon

Man with girls grinding corn (Edward S. Curtis, c. 1904).

VISITOR INFORMATION

Welcome to Hopi Land.

We want to ensure that your visit to Hopi is a pleasant experience as well as a meaningful and a memorable one. In that regard, we provide some general remarks and guidelines.

The religious and cultural activities that you may be permitted to witness are not for entertainment. All Hopi ceremonies are highly spiritual in content and should be viewed and respected as such. As with all deeply religious activities in any culture, it requires extensive preparation to accomplish the religious and ceremonial mission. Hopi philosophy teaches that life is very special and important, and that each person must be given an opportunity to offer heartfelt prayers during public viewing of these spiritual events. This is the most spiritually powerful way to focus people's energies to accomplish the ceremonial mission. Accordingly, as a guest, you are expected to show appropriate behavior, respect, and courtesy. Your positive influences and prayers will strengthen and benefit all life forms and all things in the world, which is the ceremonial purpose.

PROPER ATTIRE Dress neatly to be presentable. Women should wear dresses which are at least knee-length, or long pants and blouses. Men should wear long pants and shirts. Hats and umbrellas are considered disrespectful. DO NOT WEAR SHORTS. Shoes are required.

OTHER GUIDELINES   Photography, sketching, tape recording, and videotaping are not permitted. If you are caught doing any of these activities, your cameras/video equipment, tape recorders, and materials will be confiscated, and you will be asked to leave. No one should have to divert attention from the ceremony to deal with a visitor's disrespectful behavior. Behavior of this type has been so frequent that closure of many ceremonies to non-Indians has resulted.

These remarks and guidelines are brought to your attention because we as Hopi people want you to have a pleasant experience and enjoy your visit to Hopi Land. *Guidelines provided courtesy of Hopi Fine Arts and Alph Secakuku, Snake Clan, Shipaulovi Village*

Rim, then turns northwest toward Bill Williams Mountain, before continuing back to the Grand Canyon.

ANCIENT CULTURE

The Hopi have developed a sophisticated if precarious existence based on agriculture. Today this is evidenced by the Hopi religion, which places a strong emphasis on the land and the cycles of the seasons, both of which are intricately connected to farming and religion as a way of spiritual life.

As a culture, the early Hopi people developed innovations in ceramic and textile design. Cotton, turquoise, and other exotic materials were incorporated in the crafts. Other materials, including macaw feathers and seashells, were imported from central Mexico and the coasts of Texas and California. This is a prime example of the trade network that was established and gives us a glimpse into its level of sophistication.

FIRST EUROPEAN CONTACT

The Hopi were firmly established on the mesas by A.D. 1540, when the Spanish conquistador Coronado arrived at the village of Awat'ovi. The first contact with members of another race was cause for celebration, as the prophecy of the coming of Pahana, or the white man, had been realized. However, the Spanish were not in fact the Pahana of the prophecy, and the celebration was short-lived, as this marked the beginning of perhaps the most difficult time for the Hopi people.

At the beginning, contact with the Spanish was infrequent, as the Hopi lived on the periphery of the Spanish province of Nuevo México. During this time, sheep, cattle, horses, pigs, chickens, and

Trail to Walpi (Forman Hanna, c. 1917–39).

burros were introduced. Also, many exotic fruits and vegetables including peaches, apricots, apples, carrots, and radishes became a regular part of the Hopi diet.

However, of all the introductions being made at the time, the concept of God and the Roman Catholic Church were to have the deepest effect. In 1629, the Franciscan order established a church at

Village of Sichomovi, First Mesa (Jo Mora, c. 1904–06).

Awat'ovi in the name of the Inquisition. For the following fifty years, the Inquisition would suppress the Hopi religion and ceremonial practices. They disrespectfully mistreated and abused the Hopi and endeavored to convert the Hopi to the Catholic religion.

THE PUEBLO REVOLT

Outraged at their treatment by the Spanish, the Hopi wholeheartedly joined a movement to overthrow their oppressors. This manifested itself in the Pueblo Revolt of 1680. The Hopi people and the Pueblo people of what is now New Mexico revolted against the Spanish and drove them back into Mexico.

Fearing retaliation, the Hopi moved their low-lying villages onto the mesa tops. This is why all primary Hopi villages are at their lofty locales. Incidentally, this is also why Oraibi is considered the oldest continually inhabited village. It was founded in its present location, so no move was necessary.

This is not the case with Shungopavi, the mother village. It had been the first to be established and was originally founded at the base of West Wing of Second Mesa. It was reestablished at its present location because that was more defensible. These radical precautions were well founded. The Spanish returned and in 1692 re-conquered the Rio Grande Pueblos. They did not, however, reconquer the Hopi, as they were regarded too difficult to subdue for such an insignificant gain.

AWAT'OVI

The Franciscans, however, were hoping for another chance to reestablish themselves and eventually gained approval in Awat'ovi. In 1699 the church was reestablished. This upset many Hopi in other villages because they did not approve of the oppressive foreign influence. In 1701 Awat'ovi was sacked. Other Hopi villages attacked Awat'ovi for accepting the Spanish back. In what can simply be deemed the darkest point in modern Hopi history, warriors from all the villages, with the notable exception of Shungopavi, destroyed Awat'ovi and many of its citizens. The refugees were distributed among the villages, except for Shungopavi, and the Catholic influence was finally eliminated.

One Spanish legacy was to persist, however: smallpox. Introduced at the time of contact, the disease devastated the Hopi population in the years following, and at one point a mere 800 Hopi people remained.

Man entering kiva (Emry Kopta, c. 1912–22).

ATHAPASKANS

At or near the beginning of this entire ordeal, the Athapaskan cultures of North America were migrating south. These cultures included the Navajo and Apache people, and their arrival introduced a new kind of relationship to the Hopi people. As a nomadic, scavenging—as it was referred to by the Hopi—and gathering culture, the Athapaskans were dramatically different in their economics and mentality. Conflict soon arose out of these lifestyle and philosophical differences.

Pueblo and Spanish villages alike fell victim to raiding parties, and all suffered significant losses in crops and lives. During Spanish rule, protecting people was the responsibility of the conquistadors, who were marginal, at best, in their duties. After 1821, the newly formed Mexican government took control but did not take an active role in controlling the raids.

With the introduction of the horse, the Navajo had become much more efficient in their raids. This led to increased animosity between the two peoples as the Navajo were taking not only food and material goods, but also Hopi women and children, the most sacred people in Hopi culture. Things were to remain in this manner until the American government took control after the Treaty of

Guadalupe Hidalgo in 1848. This brought an altogether new culture into the picture.

AMERICANS

The American government was more active in its participation in the Hopi and Navajo conflict. This led the government to conclude

Village of Mishongnovi, Second Mesa (Edward S. Curtis, c. 1904).

that the Navajo were a problem that needed to be eliminated. This problem was addressed in 1863 by the U.S. Army under the command of Gen. James Henry Carleton and Col. Kit Carson, who in the bitter cold of winter forced the Navajo people to walk to a military reservation in New Mexico, in the infamous "Long Walk." This forced march decimated the Navajo, as many of the young and old died from exhaustion or exposure. A concentration camp

was established at Bosque Redondo in New Mexico to contain the Navajo. In 1868 a treaty agreement was made and the Navajo were given a portion of land by executive order. Shortly thereafter, the Navajo returned to the land that they consider their home.

This situation was further complicated in 1882, when Congress, under President Chester A. Arthur, sought to resolve the

Firing pottery, First Mesa (Kate Cory, c. 1905–12).

Navajo-Hopi conflict by designating an Executive Order Reservation for the Hopi people. The Navajo people, however, continued to settle on this reservation, despite its designation by the U.S. government.

In the 1970s the U. S. government enacted the Joint Use Area and ultimately the Partitioned Lands. This was viewed as inadequate by most Hopi, as they have retained only a fraction of their ancestral land and the Navajo lands have expanded considerably. The conflict is still sensitive to all parties involved.

As the Hopi way of life continues to experience the influence of foreign ideas, the people continue their pursuit of regaining their ancestral allotment. Currently the Hopi are using science and archaeology as tools in establishing land claims. It is for these and some religious reasons that archaeological sites have such significance to the Hopi people.

THE PRESENT DAY

The essence of Hopi life can be traced by its history. While not always consistent in its manner, Hopi life has endured because of its ability to produce adaptive strategies that keep it relevant in spite of foreign influences. The Hopi have been taught to live in the present and to base their decisions on future implications. The Hopi way of life is one that is shared by all, appreciated by few outside of the Hopi culture, and seldom understood by those who are not Hopi. The Hopi people continue to practice their ancient religion up to this day because it is a strong link to their ancient history and land and because of its instructions from the supreme being that the Hopi people call Masau, the equivalent of God.

THE HOPI HOUSEHOLD

The basic economic unit of production and consumption has always been the household. It is here that the basic division of labor between men's and women's work, between male and female property, is focused.

A man contributes his work, his fruit, his livestock, or income to whatever house he is living in: his wife's when he is married, his mother's before marriage, or his mother's or sister's if he should be divorced. Traditionally, the family was of the extended matrilineal type. By the mid-twentieth century, when it became easier to build a house or have it built, young couples began to move into houses of their own. As a result, about one-half of the families today are nuclear in pattern, with the other half reflecting the extended matrilineal pattern.

While the effect of contact with the larger society upon the Hopi economy and culture is similar in all villages, the extent is variable.

FOOD

Every Hopi house has a set of three grinding stones, set in wooden frames. These *metates* differ in the degree of coarseness. When corn is ground, it is first shelled and cracked, and then ground successively on each of the metates until it is a fine powder. Since almost all Hopi foodstuffs are made of it, plaques piled high with cornmeal are one of the most common forms of payment in exchanges between households.

Piki maker (Edward S. Curtis, c. 1904).

Grinding corn (Emry Kopta, c. 1912–22).

GRINDING CORN

Traditionally, the maternal grandmother started teaching young girls to grind corn at an early age, so they would be able to grind without assistance during the puberty ceremony, and to prepare them for their essential roles as homemakers and mothers. One essential item of equipment is the *piki* stone, sometimes located in a back room, but more often in a small house built for the purpose.

Piki is a wafer-thin bread of finely ground blue cornmeal. A fire is built under the stone. The stone surface is then rubbed with the oil from cotton seeds or watermelon seeds, and a thin batter is spread upon the stone by hand. Many houses also have a stone and adobe beehive-shaped oven outside, which is used for baking bread.

FOOD PREPARED FOR CEREMONIES

There are many ceremonial dishes prepared from a corn base, including piki and a sweet pudding called *pikomi*. A standard feast dish is hominy and mutton stew. The women prepare the hominy and the men butcher sheep, which are then cooked together. Child-naming on the twentieth day of life, a girl's corn-grinding following the first menses, marriage, and a boy's initiation, as well as all the ceremonies of the annual cycle, all require the preparation of these foods.

At marriage a girl spends four days grinding and making piki at her mother-in-law's house. Meanwhile, the men who are relatives of the groom are carding and spinning cotton and setting up a loom in a kiva to make the bride's wedding clothes. Until the weaving is finished, the bride stays grinding and cooking. When the clothes are finished, she is dressed in them and returns to her own house

accompanied by her mother-in-law, bearing a bowl of hominy stew. After they feast, her mother-in-law's bowl is filled with other Hopi foods as a gift. Later the girl and her mother and another female relative will grind and prepare other kinds of food, which is carried to the house of every man who participated in the weaving.

When a boy has his first Wuwuchim (manhood ceremony), his mother gives ground meal, piki, and other food to his ceremonial father's sister. A woman who sponsors a kachina dance is obligated to prepare food to feed all the dancers as well as the guests who will visit the house.

CLOTHING

The giving of clothing among the Hopi people had, before the introduction of manufactured goods, been ritualized into complex patterns. Social and ceremonial obligations between both individuals and clans were marked by such gifts. Articles of clothing were given to individuals at birth and when they reached some milestone in their lives such as initiation, puberty, or marriage. The assumption of a particular piece of clothing indicated passage from one social state to another.

Modern piki maker Elizabeth Tootsie.

Garments were made and conferred upon another by particular individuals who held some special relationship to the recipient, such as father, uncle, godfather, or clan relative. Great importance was attached to the initial gift. All other pieces of the same kind of clothing could then be made by anyone and used without further ceremony. Even the first article of clothing could be utilized for another purpose once it had been properly presented.

Kachina sash.

In addition to being markers of age and sex, some clothing marked the induction into societies or ritual groups. Still other items of clothing were worn only by individuals who performed specific duties. Regardless of the age of a person who died, the attire he was buried in would indicate to the inhabitants of the underworld his exact social and ceremonial standing, just as it did in the real physical world. The beginnings of this pattern are unknown as yet, but they lie far back in time, as cotton textiles have been in use for nearly two millennia. Burials, caches of material, and murals have all shown garments similar to those worn by the Hopi, in use for at least a thousand years.

CHANGES IN DRESS

The advent of the first Spanish goods some four hundred years ago began the disruption of this pattern, and the arrival of American manufactured items has continued this trend. Men's ordinary apparel was the first to succumb, probably because as travelers men were first to encounter new garments and could re-supply the items more easily.

Clothing demands of the schools of the late 1880s forced changes on the young. By 1900, a few traditional men still wore the

Spanish split-legged pants and a simple shirt. The other men, and all of the older boys and girls who had been to school, were wearing garb equivalent to their Anglo-American neighbors. The women, the very old men, and the very young retained their traditional clothing. Today only a few ultra-conservative Hopi women wear the old-style clothing on a daily basis, although more will wear it for ceremonial occasions.

Ceremonial dress, on the other hand, has been retained almost intact, although there are curious inroads here and there.

Atu-öh, **Maiden Shawl**   Formerly, this red and white blanket, the atu-öh or maiden shawl, was woven of wool and worn almost exclusively in ceremonies. This form was replaced in the ceremonies by one made of cotton with woolen borders, and the all-woolen one was relegated to secular purposes. The atu-öh is worn by the women in such ceremonies as the Mumzraud, O'waqole, and Loh kone (women's ceremonies).

Wuti Tochi, **Women's Moccasins**   Hopi women used to wear moccasins every day, but now they are usually used only on special occasions. The foot of the *Mö.Öng Tochi,* or bride's moccasin, is small and stylish. One-half of a tanned white deerskin is sewn to the

sole and wrapped about the leg to the knee, making the feet appear even tinier and giving the legs a pillar-like appearance. The footwear is presented to the bride by the relatives of the groom, presumably the only time that she ever receives these moccasins. The shoes are nearly always pure white, but today occasionally the soles are black.

Maiden shawl.

‖ HOPI ECONOMY AND SUBSISTENCE ‖

The economy of the Hopi people can be understood historically. The prehistoric foundation was an agriculture based upon the cultivation of corn, beans, squash, gourds, and cotton. During the sixteenth and seventeenth centuries, the Hopi acquired from the Spaniards domesticated animals—horses, mules, burros, sheep, and cattle. From the same source they derived peaches and apricots. Chile peppers from Mexico were also produced during this time. The period of American contact, which dates from 1849, has been marked by gradual but accelerating additions of a wide variety of consumer goods, new skills, and a cash economy, first supplementing and later displacing the traditional subsistence economy.

CROPS

The Hopi plant several varieties of corn, classified by color, but most of the fields are devoted to blue and white. They also cultivate a short-eared variety of Hopi corn. The first planting occurs in April, usually on dune fields close to the mesas, so that it will be mature by the time of the *Niman* ceremony in mid-July. The main planting, which is marked by the Bear Clan people's first planting, usually begins in the middle of May and frequently extends through the middle of June. Some men plant their fields by themselves, but others have a work party for planting (a traditional form of synergy). The men all assemble at the host's field and complete the planting in a day. In the evening when they return to the village, the host's wife feeds them all a meal in appreciation.

Sweet corn is baked in field pits and then stored for future use. Most of the corn crop is harvested in October—picked, husked, and hauled to the villages in wagons and trucks, or by burros in the old way. It is sorted by color and stored in the rear rooms of the houses, stacked like cordwood.

Stacked corn (Emry Kopta, c. 1912–22).

The Hopi grow twenty-three varieties of beans, some quite old. Several species of squash, pumpkins, and melons are regularly cultivated. The squash is dried and preserved, but the melons are eaten when they are ripe in August and September. Hopi farmers plant gourds in the same fields as squash. Gourds are used for spoons, dippers, cups, rattles, pottery scrapers, medicine containers, and as decorations.

Fruit trees do not yield a crop every year. Frequently, a late frost when the trees are in blossom destroys the potential for fruit; however, in good years they yield bountifully and most of the fruit is preserved by drying. Peaches and apricots are pitted, split in half, and spread out on top of roofs to dry. Orchards or even individual trees are owned by men. It is the tree and not the land on which it grows that is conceived to be the property, and it is inherited by men, usually sons of the previous owners.

AGRICULTURE AND LAND TENURE

Each village is autonomous and has its own land. The cultivated fields of one are separated from another by sight lines and geographic features, projected southward from the mesas. Along the watercourses below the mesas, the fields of each village are divided into sections assigned to the various matrilineal clans of the village.

Formerly, each clan allotment was marked by boundary stones. Within each clan allotment, fields are assigned to women of the clan, and they are planted and cultivated by the men of the household—husbands, brothers, or sons.

With the pattern of matrilineal inheritance and matrilineal residence, fields tend to become associated with specific households.

Leslie Koyawena weeding corn.

Each clan has land in more than one location so that if one crop fails, either from lack of rain or from sudden flooding that destroys the crop, the other may still be productive. Formerly, some fields were allocated to the ceremonial societies' leaders, but this custom has disappeared. In addition, any man may establish a field in the area beyond clan land holdings. He has the right to use it; however, should he abandon it, that land reverts to the common domain.

The possession of horses and wagons, and later pickup trucks, facilitated the development of more distant fields. Hopi agriculture has always been precarious, subject to long-term wet and dry cycles. In the period from 1866 to 1870 there was a nearly total crop failure, and some villages were abandoned while the people sought refuge with the pueblos to the east. In a study of land use in the Oraibi Valley, it was discovered that the natural rerouting of the wash had over a period of fifty years destroyed approximately one-third of the fields that had been in cultivation.

There is no private property in grazing land. Horses and burros are hobbled and permitted to graze where they will. Cattle are permitted to drift in areas where there is a relatively permanent supply of water. Sheep are herded every day and corralled at night. Most sheep owners have shelters or regular Hopi houses in the area where they customarily graze their sheep. Sometimes they have their major cornfields in the same area in places like Coyote Spring and Burro Spring.

Irrigated gardens watered from nearby springs are utilized for the cultivation of chile peppers, onions, and other vegetables, and titles to these small plots are jealously guarded. A Potki clan plot below Wepo Spring was planted every year by men from Shungopavi, whose grandmother had come from Tewa Village on First Mesa.

Although the pattern of land ownership is clear in Hopi theory and reflects the myths of the settlement of each village, adjustments sometimes have to be made. Matrilineages vary in size and can increase or decrease in a few generations. Should there be a shortage of land in his wife's clan lands, a man may be assigned a few of his own clan lands, or his father's, if there is a surplus.

WILD PLANTS

The Hopi make extensive use of wild plants in their habitat, utilizing 134 of the 150 local plant species. For example, the roots of yucca (soapweed) are used in hair washing, which is an essential part of every ceremony—naming, initiation, girl's puberty, grinding, and marriage. Yucca leaves are split and sewn around a core in making coiled basketry and in making sifting baskets and trays.

The Hopi brush, which is an essential tool in every house, is made from clumps of purple hair grass. A handful is tied with a piece

of string near the butt end. The shorter end can serve as a hairbrush, and this tool is also used to sweep the meal from the grinding stones, as well as to sweep the floor of houses with adobe floors.

HUNTING

Hunting has been traditionally important. The area is not rich in large game, although deer and antelope were reported to have grazed in the area between the Hopi buttes and the Little Colorado River. They were formerly hunted by men in pairs, and taken and prepared in the traditional way by making *pahos* (prayer feathers).

Rabbit hunting is a regular form of small game hunting throughout the year. In the announcement of the hunt, the place names along the route of the hunt and the route of return are all included. In the morning the men assemble with their throwing sticks. They form a "circle" a mile to a mile and a half wide, and begin shrinking the circle, those at the rear closing it up. When a rabbit is raised the hunters throw their sticks at it with a sideways arm motion. When a man hits and stuns a rabbit, he runs to it and kills it, by hand.

Hazel Dukepoo arranges Carol Dawahoya's hair in the traditional butterfly whorl or maiden style.

LIVESTOCK

Sheep and cattle are the major forms of men's property. Horses, burros, and wagons also become important as the distance one has to travel to his fields or to cut and haul firewood increases. The size of the flocks and herds has always been limited by the amount of browse and the availability of water.

From the earliest days of the agency at Keams Canyon, the U.S. government made systematic efforts to aid the Hopi stockmen. Drilling deep wells with windmills, storage tanks, and watering troughs has been one of the most effective ways of aiding the growth of the Hopi herds. Efforts were also made to improve herd quality by assisting in the purchase of purebred rams and bulls.

Sheep owners usually have one or two partners—a pair of brothers, father and son, uncle and nephew. A man will spend two or three days at a time herding and then be relieved by his partner. Men who have corrals close to the mesa pen their sheep at night and go out to herd each day. During the lambing season all hands are with the flock, and each earmarks the lambs from his own ewes. In June the flocks are brought close to the village, and work parties assemble to shear the sheep. The wool clip is sold to the traders,

Village of Old Oraibi, Third Mesa (Jo Mora, c. 1904–06).

and until the end of World War II this was often the only source of money for many men.

Most Hopi do not sell their lambs; they are butchered and eaten on all the occasions during the year that require feasts, such as dance days, weddings, and initiations. They practically never butcher just to have meat in their diet. What little is not cooked for the immediate occasion is dried in the sun and preserved for future use.

Cattle are always marketed. With the spread of wage work and other forms of cash income on the reservation since 1946, the Hopi people have been shifting their forms of livestock from sheep to cattle, which do not require constant care. At the same time, the widespread ownership of cars and trucks has reduced the need for horses and burros, freeing that many more range units for cattle.

TRADE

The Hopi people have traded with the Navajo for sheep and wool, with the Havasupai for buckskin, and with the Zuni and the eastern Pueblo people for turquoise and other goods. Hopi weavers of ceremonial garments have kept the other Pueblo people supplied for many years.

A trading post at Keams Canyon was opened in 1881, and Hubbell's post at Oraibi was established in 1919. All other posts and stores on the reservation have been owned and managed by Hopi people; many have been started, operated for a number of years, and then abandoned. Tom Pavatea's post at Polacca was one of the largest and most successful. When he died in 1941, his estate was valued at more than $40,000, a small fortune at that time.

Clothing, flour, sugar, coffee, and canned goods were sold at the trading posts, and craft products, corn, and wool were taken in payment as well as money when it was available. With the spread of wage work, both on and off the reservation, and with the completion of a network of paved roads in the 1960s, a cash economy

Wicker wedding basket, Third Mesa.

has been gradually displacing the traditional subsistence economy. As a result, trading posts have become supermarkets. Bottled gas, electricity, and refrigeration permit the sale of fresh meat, frozen vegetables, fruit, and a multiplicity of other foodstuffs.

HOPI ARTS AND CRAFTS

A supplementary source of income in every household is the production of crafts. Since the beginning of the twentieth century, women's products have tended to become specialized; at First Mesa they make pottery; at Second Mesa, coiled baskets; and at Third Mesa, wicker baskets.

Hopi men do the textile weaving, and the bulk of their work is in ceremonial garments of cotton and wool. Sashes, kilts, wedding robes, belts, and garters are the most commonly produced forms of the weaver's art. They also make the woolen black dress, or *manta,* which is part of a woman's traditional costume, and knit black or blue leggings, which are worn in dances.

Third Mesa wicker plaque.

The carving and painting of kachina dolls has become increasingly popular with the growth of a cash economy. Originally they were never meant to be sold; they were made for distribution by kachinas to girls at dances, but they are now made in large numbers for sale in the market. They tend to become larger and more elaborately carved and feathered to appeal to the tastes of the buyers.

POTTERY

The most abundant cultural artifacts remaining from prehistoric occupation are pottery. Beautifully decorated and technically excellent, potsherds demonstrate an early mastery of the ceramic art. The same tradition continues to the present with only a minor degeneration in the 1800s.

The renaissance of fine pottery is credited to a Tewa-Hopi woman named Nampeyo (c. 1859–1942). She copied the designs of prehistoric ancestral pottery when it was collected in the 1890s from the excavation at the Sikyatki ruins below First Mesa. Nampeyo, noted as a ceramic artist, learned the craft from her Hopi grandmother. Such learning habits and intermarriage have welded the pottery traditions of First Mesa into a single unity. In earlier times all of the villages on the three mesas made pottery, although today some have lost the art entirely, while others such as Oraibi and Hotevilla still have a few women and men who produce it.

Hopi pottery is made entirely by hand, using only the simplest tools: a piece of gourd for scraping, a pebble for smoothing, and a yucca-leaf paintbrush.

HISAT CHAKAFTA, HISTORIC POTTERY

Black-on-white (to 1200) The earliest decorated pottery in the Southwest is the Black-on-white ware. Although different regional styles were developed, Black-on-white was made all over the Southwest.

Kayenta Polychrome (1200–1300) The distinctive Black-on-red and Black-on-white-on-red polychrome pottery was developed in the Kayenta region of Northern Arizona. The red background color is a slip of thin clay spread over the pot. The actual color of the paste is yellow-orange.

Klagtoh Black-on-white mugs (c. 1200).

Nampeyo (Edward S. Curtis, c. 1904).

Jeddito Black-on-yellow (1300–1600) Some time in the fourteenth century, the red slip of Kayenta Polychrome was dropped in favor of black and white decorations directly on the yellow paste.

Sikyatki Polychrome (1300–1600) The ultimate expression of the flowing designs begun on Jeddito yellow wares is Sikyatki Polychrome. The conventionalized life forms show a striking flamboyance of decoration and design unequaled in the previous styles. Sikyatki Polychrome represents the height of prehistoric Hopi ceramic art.

Sikyatki polychrome jar.

Polacca Polychrome (1850–1900) In the middle of the nineteenth century, a drought and smallpox epidemic forced some Hopi families to move to Zuni Pueblo, New Mexico. When they returned, they brought many of the traits of Zuni pottery, including the use of a white slip, and many design elements.

Tsegi Red-on-orange serving ladle (c. A.D. 1200).

Jeddito Black-on-yellow bowl (c. 1300–1600).

CONTEMPORARY POTTERY

Contemporary Hopi pottery is based upon a long and proud tradition, which has continued to flourish since pre-Columbian times. A Hopi pot, like most Pueblo pottery, is made by the coil method. First ropes of clay are formed and then spiraled around and around, one on top of another. The surface is smoothed, the pot is dried, and a coat of slip (watery clay) is smoothed onto the surface. The slip is then polished with a smooth stone, a design is painted on or incised, and the piece is then fired. The firing process begins with the placing of the pots on a grate and then covering them with broken potsherds; dried manure is placed all around and then burned.

One type of Hopi pottery is a decorated yellow-orange ware after the style of the distinguished Tewa-Hopi potter Nampeyo. A white clay pottery with designs is also popular, as is a type made from red clay with a white slipped interior.

JEWELRY

Jewelry making is an art that has been practiced for many centuries by the Hopi people and other Pueblo Indians of the Southwest.

Through the use of bone, shell, turquoise, stone, wood, leather, and even basketry, prehistoric jewelry took on many forms. The earliest Spanish explorers entering Arizona reported being met by people wearing feather headdresses, strings of beads, bracelets, and ear pendants. Excavations of prehistoric sites have uncovered such jewelry in both quantity and quality.

Silver bolo tie.

Silver and turquoise bracelet.

It was not until the coming of the Spaniards, during the 1500s, that metal was used as jewelry, and the introduction of silver brought about a new era of Pueblo jewelry making. Around 1938, due to encouragement primarily by the Museum of Northern Arizona in Flagstaff, the Hopi began to develop a style of their own. This was done by combining pottery designs with the overlay process.

Before 1946, there were a few Hopi silversmiths, but their work was not distinguishable from that of the Navajo or Zuni. In 1947 two Hopi men developed a silversmith school for a group of Hopi veterans of World War II, and a set of traditional Hopi design elements was adapted to the possibilities of the medium. In 1949, they established a guild with its own hallmark. On

Copper preliminary model for silverwork.

Second Mesa, at the junction of Piñon and Highway 264, the Hopi Arts and Crafts Guild now has its own building, where native products are displayed and sold. Any craftsman, potter, basketmaker, weaver, or silversmith can have his or her work displayed and sold there. Half of the building is devoted to work benches and supplies for the silversmiths.

OTHER CRAFTS

Lightning Sticks The lightning stick is a dancing wand, used in social dances such as the Buffalo Dance.

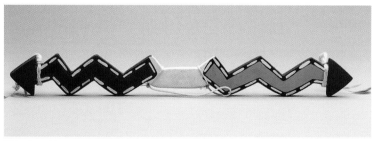

Lightning stick.

Aya, **Rattles** Rattles are important Hopi musical instruments because of the importance of rhythm. There are a number of varieties of rattles made from gourds, hooves, turtle shells, metal, and seashells.

KACHINAS AND HOPI RELIGION

Kachina religion is very complex. It relates to society as a whole because it involves more than just the kachina dances that people normally see when there is a public dance, and there are various types of kachinas—some are private, some make public appearances, and some are clan gods or idols that members of a clan hold very sacred and pray to.

Aya, Rattles.

KACHINAS

Each of the carved figures known as kachina dolls represents a kachina spirit who appears in religious dances.

As spirits, the kachinas are supernatural beings who visit the Hopi villages during the first half of every year and are believed to live on any high peaks surrounding the Hopi during the rest of the year. They come to the Hopi villages to sing and dance, bring gifts for the children, and above all to bring rain.

The total number of kachinas known to the Hopi is estimated at over 250. It seems that there are fads in kachinas, for once-popular characters have disappeared and new characters are frequently invented. Some kachinas appear every year, while some are rarely seen. Moreover, the customs and bearing of the same kachina may vary from village to village.

Every kachina has a name. Some have the names of birds or animals; for example, the Eagle Kachina and the Bear Kachina. Others

have descriptive names—the Left-Handed and Red Beard Kachinas—and others may be known by special features such as a call or noise, such as Hu Kachinas or Ho-ote. Still others have Hopi names for which there are no English equivalents, such as Eototo.

There are many cult groups in the Hopi villages, but the kachina cult differs from all the rest. Most of the Hopi men and some of the women are members, and every initiated man takes part in kachina ceremonies through his life; if he lives off the reservation, he usually returns for the kachina ceremonies.

Owl kachina.

Kachina carvings at the Hopi Cultural Center Museum.

ADDITIONAL DEITIES

In addition to the kachinas, the Hopi recognize over thirty supreme beings who might be called deities (such as the god of the sky, So'tuknang-u, and the earth god, Masau).

Also, there is another distinct type of kachina called Chief Kachinas, who appear only at specific times and never dance in groups.

KACHINA DANCES

Hopi religious ceremonies take place in a set order, based on solar and lunar observations, but the kachina dances are performed only between the winter solstice and July. The *Powamuya* or Bean Dance in February and the Niman or Home Dance in July are the two major

Buffalo Dance (a social, not a kachina dance) at Hano village, First Mesa (Edward S. Curtis, c. 1904).

ceremonies in the kachina cult. In addition, kachinas appear in night dances in the kivas during February and March. With the coming of milder weather, the kachinas dance outside in the village plaza.

KACHINAS AND HOPI RELIGIOUS PRACTICES

From the winter solstice to midsummer, roughly the first half of each year, the religious practices of the Hopi people are focused on kachinas and the ceremonials connected with these important spirits. In performing rituals of song and dance, male members of the kachina societies portray ancestor spirits and spirits of the animals, plants, and other objects in the Hopi natural world. In ceremonies held according to the moon's cycle, kachinas make appearances in the Hopi villages to help the people perform their ceremonial duties—the basis of the Hopi way of life. When the kachinas leave the windswept, high desert mesas of Hopi in northeastern Arizona and return to their "homes" in the San Francisco Peaks north of Flagstaff, other ceremonials continue but kachinas are not seen, except as intricately carved representations.

Water serpent kachina.

Carvings of kachinas were originally intended for the children of the villages. The wooden figures were among presents given to young people during the Bean Dance ceremonies, Powamuya, to be used as part of their spiritual training. Today, while the annual kachina ceremonies continue the ancient traditions and certain kachinas are still present during Powamuya, many more carvings are apparent. These are contemporary art pieces, treasured for their magnificent workmanship as well as their reflections of Hopi ceremonials.

EAGLES

Since before the coming of the white man, the Hopi people have used the feathers of eagles and other birds in religious ceremonies. The feathers are used in making pahos to carry blessings from the Hopi people to the Cloud People and the sacred spiritual world. During the winter solstice, or *Soyalung,* pahos are deposited at the traditional prayer shrines, with prayers and blessings for the eagles. In the spring, visits are made to the eagle nesting sites, some of which are as far south as Meteor Crater, eighty miles away. In early summer, the young men again visit the nesting sites to get the young eagles.

The young eagles are treated like newborn children. On the trip back to the village, they are carried in special cradleboards. The next morning, their heads are washed and they are given clan names. A shelter is built on the clan housetop for the eagles, and they are cared for by the young men of the house. Daily they go out hunting and fishing for fresh meat—rabbits and other small game.

By midsummer, the eagles are fully grown. At this time, the kachinas come to the village to dance for the last time before they depart for their homes on the San Francisco Peaks. During the breaks in the dancing, all children in the village, including the eagles, are given presents by the Niman Kachinas. The sharp cries of the eagles on the rooftops can be heard throughout the day as the kachinas dance, and each cry adds blessings to the day's activities.

Early in the morning of the day after Niman, the eagles are brought into their clan houses. Here the clan elders gather and make a prayer to the eagles. The elders tell the eagles that the Hopi will use their feathers in the ceremonies, and for pahos, to give prayers from the Hopi to all sacred beings. The eagles are then smothered in cornmeal. The feathers are carefully saved and preserved for future use, while the bodies are buried in a special eagle cemetery outside the village.

SOYOKOS

Soyokos are disciplinary kachinas who come to some villages either during the Powamuya ceremony or immediately thereafter. About a week before the Soyokos are to appear, either Soyoko Wu-ti, Hahai-ih, or Soyoko Mana and an attendant appear and go through the village, pausing at each house. The Soyokos tell the children they must catch small game or grind corn against the time when they will return. Each boy is given a yucca snare and told to catch small game. Each girl is given corn to grind into cornmeal.

Ceremony with Soyoko group, Walpi (James Mooney, 1893). Courtesy of National Anthropological Archives, Smithsonian Institution.

A few days later they return with a great group of Soyoko Kachinas, which consist of the mother, grandmother, uncles, Soyoko Mana, and brothers.

Approaching the house, the Soyokos demand meat, and all small trapped game or sweet cornmeal must then be proffered as a meager ransom to the growling, stomping group. Regardless of what is offered, it is indignantly refused and more food demanded lest they take the child. To add weight to their demands they recount the misbehavior of the children, telling how they don't mind and are no help to their parents. Any petty misdeed that is brought up is countered by a relative who points out that the child has really learned his lesson and no longer makes such mistakes. They then offer other food to the Soyokos in place of the children. Eventually the Soyokos go clacking and grumbling away to pile their goods in the kiva.

At the end of the day the men of the village lure the Soyokos into a dance on some pretext, and then while the Soyokos are thoroughly involved in learning the dance the men suddenly leap upon them and wrest from them all of their ill-gotten gains. Deprived of everything, they are driven from the village.

The children, who are involved at every step, learn a series of object lessons. They must contribute to the food supply or die. Their well-being is dependent on the goodwill of their relatives, and the village men will protect its inhabitants.

‖ THE HOPI YEAR ‖

Powamuya, **The Moon of Purification (February)** The lunar month of Powamuya marks the beginning of kachina dances, which start with the Bean Dance. Preparation and growth are the central attributes of this ceremony: preparation of the young people of the villages for initiation into the kachina societies, concern for their growth and development, and, in a parallel sense, preparation of the earth for planting and concern for the growth of corn, beans, and squash—the traditional Hopi crops. Powamuya also incorporates a purifying ceremony performed for all things animate and inanimate, not only in the immediate Hopi environment but throughout the entire world. In this month matrimonial events also take place.

Late at night, the kachinas appear in the kivas, relating the history and philosophy of the Hopi, including the coming of the Moon Kachina, who plays a vital role during Powamuya and all ceremonies in this Moon of Purification.

Ösömuyu, **The Moon of Low Whistling Sounds (March)** The Hopi people do not distinguish between the kachina and the spirit it represents; upon participation, the two become one. Every village has its own kachinas. For the Night Kiva Dances, *Angwa,* held during this and subsequent months, each group selects the specific rituals it will perform, dancing first in its home kiva. Then each group dances for the other kivas, returning for a final performance in the home kiva at the end of the night. Gifts are always given out at every dance site. The rigorous Night Kiva Dances, also known as Repeat Dances, are performed to encourage ancestors in the spirit world to return as clouds, bringing needed moisture to the dry land.

The Repeat Dances are announced by a pair of Mudheads, *Kooyemsi,* who tell the time and date of the dance. They also ask that special food be prepared for the kachinas. Occasionally when the weather is warmer, Repeat Dances include an outdoor plaza performance. Runner Kachinas, *Wawaskachina,* appear during the spring. They come to the villages to challenge men and young boys to race. The loser will always suffer some consequence, depending on which kachina he races. Runner Kachinas bring presents of food to distribute after each race. When the food is gone, the races end. Then the runners are sprinkled with cornmeal by village elders who ask that they, too, pray for the all-important rain.

***Pömaui,* The Moon of Preparation for Planting (April) •
Ui'yis, The Moon of Waiting (May) • *Wu ko ui yis,* The Moon of
Planting (June)** A special crop of early corn is planted as soon as
the ground is ready, in April. This will be harvested in midsummer
for the final kachina ceremonial, Niman. With the coming of
warmer and longer days, the kachinas move their dances into the
village plazas, and weeks of preparation precede each two-day plaza
dance: new songs are composed and great quantities of food prepared—including the traditional piki bread made by the women.
The kachinas dance and sing in unison, always turning together
within the complex patterns of their dances, pooling their energies
and, by extension, the energies of everyone present, to make a com-
munity of prayer. The Hopi people believe this harmony of thought
will make the spirits look favorably on the living. The ultimate purpose in asking the spirits' favors is to bring life-sustaining rain.

During the plaza dances, sacred Hopi clowns, the *Tsu'ku* or
Kooyemsi, reconstruct the human life cycle in speech and action.
With antic movements and mimicry, other groups of clowns reenact
behaviors that violate the laws of Hopi society. These clowns show
the people how not to act.

Toward the end of a plaza dance—the afternoon of the second day—kachinas warn the antic clowns to behave. The clowns, of course, ignore the warnings and so must be punished and purified. The purpose is always to show that un-Hopi or *qahopi* behavior will not be tolerated. Clowns from each village are distinguished by styles of face and body painting.

***Na'sun muyao,* The Moon of Great Power (July)** Niman, the second of the great kachina ceremonials, is held in Na'sun muyao. It marks the closure of the kachina season first begun on Second Mesa with the Bean Dance. The early corn is harvested, and the villages prepare for the departure of the kachinas, who will soon return to their "spiritual homes" in the San Francisco Peaks.

During the sixteen days of Niman, dances and songs ask the spirits' favor for rain and for guidance that will enable the young people to grow in purity, unselfishness, honesty, integrity, and love.

The Niman kachina dance, or Home Dance, honors the brides whose marriages were announced during the winter solstice ceremonies. The dignitaries of the kachina societies appear only for the two great kachina celebrations of Powamuya and Niman. Members of the Pu'wa mu'ah Society, an exclusive kachina group, bless the kachinas for the last time. The dancers receive sacred white cornmeal and prayer feathers. One of the kachina "fathers," who officiate in every ceremonial, makes a farewell speech and sends the kachinas "home."

In August come the summer and social dances, including the Butterfly Dance and Snake or Flute Dance. September and October are the months for the Women's Society activities, followed in November and December by the Men's Society activities. In January, after a short slow period, there are winter social dances, including the Buffalo Dance. That brings the year around to Powamuya or February again.

HOPI CEREMONIAL CALENDAR MURAL

This 274-square-foot mural is the first in a series of murals painted by the collective group called Artist Hopid.

Hopi Ceremonial Calendar depicts the Hopi ceremonial cycle based on the moon cycle. The mural is painted in the traditional (ca. A.D. 900–1400) Hopi mural style: flat, two-dimensional, and using earth colors. This style was used in painting kiva frescos long before the coming of Columbus and the white man.

The background colors of the mural represent the colors of the four directions: yellow for the north, green or blue the west, red the

HOPI CEREMONIAL YEAR MURAL

This mural was painted in reverence and in homage to Hopi:

A life force and philosophy that nurtured and gave strength to
countless generations of Hopi people.

A way of life, time tested by the forces of Mother Nature for eons;
survived and matured.

A concept so deep that deliberate attempts by gold and soul-hungry
ideologies to un-root it have failed.

A spiritual outlook so strong, that despite the hardships, it prays for all
living beings to have fulfilling lives,

And those beautiful souls that live its teachings, and guide it,

The Hopi people.

So with the greatest honor and respect, members of Artist Hopid
dedicate *Hopi Ceremonial Calendar* to the Hopi people, and all
living beings.

ARTIST HOPID: Delbridge Honanie (Coochsiwukioma), Michael Kabotie (Lomawywesa), Milland Lomakema (Dawakema), Terrance Talaswima (Honventewa), and Neil David (Sung'quai). Funds for this mural were granted by the Tiffany Foundation, New York, New York.

south, and white for the east. Surrounding the mural is a rainbow rising from the oceans and covering much of the earth. Against this background are painted the moons, represented by six smaller circles, each standing for two moons. Looking at the mural, the circle farthest to the left, outlined with a thin white crescent, represents the coming of a new moon; the center large circle represents the full moon, with the moon at the farthest right finishing the cycle of one lunar month.

In the center large circle or the full moon stand two deities representing the two leading clans of the Hopi: the Soyal Kachina (left), representative of the Bear Clan, and the Ahula (right), representing the Kachina Clan. Both stand atop the Sun, giver of warmth and beauty, and all are connected to the earth by a paho that is dipping into the medicine bowl, containing seeds of plants useful to mankind. The medicine bowl sits atop the land altar covering the plants and seeds that will bloom and cover the land in spring and summer.

From two ends of the mural, two cornmeal (white) lines represent the roads of life that run toward the Sun, being blessed by two Hopi priests. The priest to the right smokes sacred tobacco, and the other sprinkles cornmeal. The crooked canes represent the steps to old age. Beneath the canes the bear paws represent the migration of the Bear Clan and the other clans, with the blue pyramid clouds bringing moisture to the corn.

Bear Clan Leadership Looking at the mural from left to right, all those ceremonies that are conducted under the guidance of the Bear Clan are to the left. The circle to the farthest left, with the crescent moon, represents the month of August. During this month, most mesas perform the Snake, Antelope, and Flute ceremonies. All three ceremonies are for rain and for an abundant harvest. The Snake Ceremony is represented by both the Snake and Antelope Societies, blessing the snake. The Flute Society members are blessing the corn crops and flowers with the sweet-sounding flute.

The second circle represents the months of September and October. It is during the latter part of September that the Mumzraud (Women's Society) perform their Knee High Dances, signifying the maturity of a woman to be able to make proper prayers by painting her flesh in the sacred symbols of the prayer stick. This ceremony is represented by a female with her thighs painted in the symbols of prayer.

In October, the *Lakon* or Basket Dance is performed, with the women again doing the prayers for the preparation of the coming winter and for the wild game to be plentiful, so the men can hunt them; thus, usually within the dance there is a long-distance race. Another dimension of the ceremony is the confirmation of the young women to be weavers of a craft representing the cycle of life from birth to death: the basket. In the mural the two women are singing and dancing with baskets as the third member shares with the audience the crops that the women helped to grow through their prayers.

The next small circle directly left of the large circle represents the moons of November and December. In the last part of November, the Wuwchimt, or Men's Societies—including Sacred Song Society, One-horn Society, and Two-horn Society—are in the kiva praying for the rebirth of life. The Wuwchimt is represented in the mural by the one-horned priest.

Then in December, all members of the kiva societies are meditating in homage to the Sun, seeking in prayer for the Sun as Father to lead the people back to warmer seasons. Here Ahlusaka, the fertility priest, stands as a symbol of the Soyalung, the winter solstice. It is during the conclusion of the winter solstice that the leadership passes from the Bear Clan to the Kachina Clan. Ahula, the old Kachina Priest, is the first to make his appearance at the end of December.

Kachina Clan Leadership The first small circle to the right of the large full moon stands for the months of January and February. During January, the Hopi villages participate in the social dances, represented here by the Buffalo Dancers. This month represents the barbaric past of the Hopi people; thus singers and dancers can give loud whoops and war cries. The other side of the Melting of the Moon month is to prepare for the long journey toward summer.

Powamuya or February is the Moon of Purification. It is this month that portrays the coming of kachinas to the Hopi to purify during the Bean Dance ceremonies, and a prayer for a fertile summer. The kachinas represented in the mural are the Crow Kachina Mother, the high Priest Eototo, and the Quoklo, the storytelling friend of the children.

The next small circle to the right represents April through June, when the kachinas come with clouds to bless and entertain the people. They come with gifts and songs of goodwill. This portion is represented by kachinas arriving with the rainbow to dance in the kiva and plazas of the Hopi villages. Then again in June the priests meditate in the middle of summer for a fruitful summer. This is represented by the priest sitting in meditation, preparing prayer feathers.

July, the last circle, farthest to the right, is when the last of the kachina ceremonies takes place, the Niman Dance or the Home Dance. This kachina dance, in conjunction with the Purifying Society, again purifies the people before the kachina spirits depart for their cloud homes on the mountains, west and east. This ceremony is depicted in the mural by the Purifying Society sitting in a smoke circle and by the corn stalks, the first crop to be harvested. The Kachina Priest Eototo holds the sagebrush with which he purifies the people. The other kachinas in the picture are the Niman Kachina, crowned with cloud symbols, and the Kachina Maiden with the butterfly whorl hairdo.

With the conclusion of the Niman ceremony, the leadership is again passed to the Bear Clan to lead until the winter solstice.

NA-LAU-NANG-EVAK MURAL (THE FOUR DIRECTIONS)

Na-Lau-Nang-Evak visually captures and interprets the reverence for the spiritual powers—colors, birds, flowers, and cloud symbols—of the four directional points of the Hopi.

Center of the Universe In the center of the mural, the small circle is symbolic of the Hopi Center of the Universe. It is from this

HOPI FOUR DIRECTIONS MURAL

Na-Lau-Nang-Evak (The Hopi Four Directions) is the second mural painted by members of Artist Hopid: Coochsiwukioma, Dawakema, and Neil David; with Honventewa and Lomawywesa acting as consultants. This 130-square-foot mural was painted in *reverence* and *homage* to:

Hopi,

Its People,

Philosophy,

Spiritual Strength

and Outlook.

So again with the greatest honor and respect, members of Artist Hopid dedicate *Na-Lau-Nang-Evak* to all living things and the Hopi people.

Artist Hopid

ARTIST HOPID: Delbridge Honanie (Coochsiwukioma), Michael Kabotie (Lomawywesa), Milland Lomakema (Dawakema), Terrance Talaswima (Honventewa), and Neil David (Sung'quai).

circle that the Hopi village priestly-fathers sit in prayer and summon the spiritual beings to purify and strengthen life on this earth. The cross inside the circle points to the various directional-priestly-homes.

Directional Colors and Birds In the outer oval are painted the colors and birds associated with the various directions. Representing the North is the color yellow and the yellow finch; the West color is green-blue, and the bird is the bluebird. The South bird is the parrot and the color red; the East is symbolized by the color white, and the

bird is the sparrow. During the various ceremonies, feathers of the directional birds are used to symbolically carry the prayers to the directional-priestly-homes.

Seasonal Clouds and Plants   Painted in the oval are the seasonal clouds and the plants that grow and mature during the various seasons. At the top of the mural are the white clouds of winter that moisten the land, and upon its moisture the flowers of spring bloom. To the right of the mural are the black clouds of spring, which nourish the young plants that will be the first to mature about the end of July. The blue cumulus clouds of summer are painted at the bottom of the mural, bringing rain to the young bean sprouts, which will begin maturing in late summer. The red, blue, and yellow clouds of autumn are depicted to the left in the mural, overcasting the squash plants, which are the last of the Hopi staples to mature in late autumn, ending the seasonal cycle. It is to these various cloud-priests that the Hopi prayer is directed for the well-being of plants and for prosperity.

Day and Night   The black background represents the dark of night, when most of the esoteric religious activities and prayers take place. Day is represented by white. During this time, we awake to see the fruits of our village priestly-fathers' prayers being answered. The

Basket Dance, Walpi (Jo Mora, c. 1904–06).

four directional father-priests are represented by four figures in their most humble attire—kilts—carrying blessed holy waters to purify and strengthen life on earth. The rainbow around the edge of the

mural represents the house of the Sun, whose warmth has added beauty to the spirituality of the Hopi.

Funds for this mural were granted by the Arizona Commission on the Arts and Humanities, Phoenix, Arizona, with matching funds provided by the Hopi Cultural Center Museum and the Hopi Arts and Crafts Guild located at the "Center of the Universe," Second Mesa, Arizona.

THE END OF OUR JOURNEY

To the many people I have met in my lifetime, and to all my new readers: I hope I have touched your life in some way by sharing my cultural information with you. Thank you very much for visiting Hopi Land.

Asquoli, thank you. Come again.

Hairstyling (Edward S. Curtis, 1904).

‖ PLACES TO VISIT ‖

Arizona State Museum, University of Arizona
1013 E. University Blvd.
Tucson, Arizona
520-621-6302
www.statemuseum.arizona.edu

Canyon de Chelly National Monument
Chinle, Arizona
928-674-5500
www.nps.gov/cach/

Heard Museum
2301 N. Central Ave.
Phoenix, Arizona
602-252-8848
www.heard.org

Homolovi Ruins State Park
north of Winslow, Arizona
928-289-4106
www.pr.state.az.us/parks/parkhtml
  /homolovi.html

Hopi Arts & Crafts Silver Craft Cooperative Guild
Second Mesa, Arizona
928-734-2463

Hopi Cultural Center Museum
Second Mesa, Arizona
602-734-6650

Hubbell Trading Post National Historic Site
Ganado, Arizona
928-755-3475
www.nps.gov/hutr/

Museum of New Mexico
Museum of Indian Arts & Culture
708–710 Camino Lejo
Santa Fe, New Mexico
505-476-1250
www.museumofnewmexico.org

Museum of Northern Arizona
3101 N. Fort Valley Rd.
Flagstaff, Arizona
928-774-5213
www.musnaz.org

Navajo National Monument
Tonalea, Arizona
928-672-2710
www.nps.gov/nava

Petrified Forest National Park
1 Park Rd.
Petrified Forest, Arizona
928-524-6228
www.nps.gov/pefo/

Tuba City Trading Post
Main St. & Moenava Rd.
Tuba City, Arizona
928-283-5441

Wupatki National Monument
north of Flagstaff, Arizona
928-679-2365
www.nps.gov/wupa

Village of Mishongnovi, Second Mesa
(Jo Mora, c. 1904–06).

‖ SUGGESTED READING ‖

Courlander, Harold. *The Fourth World of the Hopis: The Epic Story of the Hopi Indians as Preserved in Their Legends and Traditions.* Albuquerque, NM: University of New Mexico Press, 1987.

James, Harry C. *Pages from Hopi History.* Tucson, AZ: University of Arizona Press, 1974.

Kosik, Frank. *Native Roads: The Complete Motoring Guide to the Navajo & Hopi Nations,* 2nd ed. Tucson, AZ: Rio Nuevo Publishers, 2005.

Qoyawayma, Polingaysi, Vada F. Carlson, and Elizabeth Q. White. *No Turning Back: A Hopi Indian Woman's Struggle to Live in Two Worlds.* Albuquerque, NM: University of New Mexico Press, 1977.

Sekaquaptewa, Helen. *Me and Mine: The Life Story of Helen Sekaquaptewa* (as told to Louise Udall). Tucson, AZ: University of Arizona Press, 1969.

Wright, Barton. *Kachinas: A Hopi Artist's Documentary.* Flagstaff, AZ: Northland Publishing, 1973.

The Hopi Cultural Center, including the museum, was designated an Arizona Treasure by Governor Janet Napolitano in 2005.

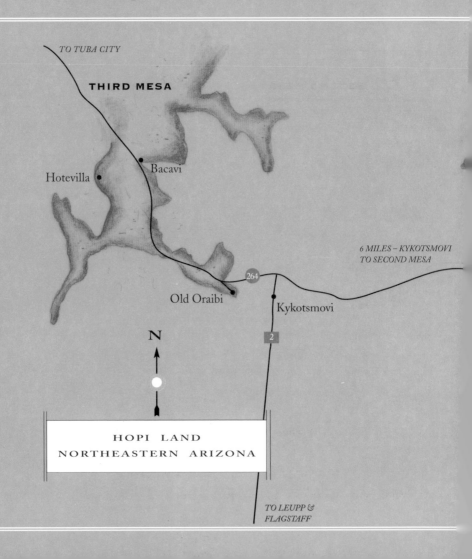

TO TUBA CITY

THIRD MESA

Hotevilla

Bacavi

*6 MILES – KYKOTSMOVI
TO SECOND MESA*

264

Old Oraibi

Kykotsmovi

N

2

HOPI LAND
NORTHEASTERN ARIZONA

*TO LEUPP &
FLAGSTAFF*